Corky
THE Wander Dog

A New Family Member

Janet DiLeo Wade

Illustrated by CHARLES SORRENTO

CORKY THE WANDER DOG
A NEW FAMILY MEMBER

iUniverse books may be ordered through booksellers or by contacting:

iUniverse
1663 Liberty Drive
Bloomington, IN 47403
www.iuniverse.com
1-800-Authors (1-800-288-4677)

ISBN: 978-1-5320-5978-0 (sc)
ISBN: 978-1-5320-5979-7 (e)

Library of Congress Control Number: 2018912288

Print information available on the last page.

iUniverse rev. date: 11/19/2018

Corky was a mutt. Actually, he was part golden retriever and part Labrador retriever, plus a few other things. But really, he was just a funny, crazy, lovable dog who felt no sense of family loyalty. He would walk off with anyone, from postmen to pretty women to punk teens to little children. He wasn't selective. He loved everyone, and everyone loved him. He was confident that regardless of whom he followed or where he went, we would eventually find him and bring him home.

Mom and Dad first found him at the pet store. They couldn't miss him. He was the big goofy dog with one ear up and one ear down, a floppy pink tongue, a happy face, and a friendly bark that said, "Come on! Let's go home!"

We four kids were at home, waiting excitedly for our new family member, when he bounded through the door. He was very affectionate. He licked all of us on our faces, our arms, and our legs. When someone sat in a chair, he would nudge his head under their hand as if to say, "Come on! Pet me! I need some lovin'."

Because Mom had recently eaten ribs at a place called Corky's Barbeque and liked the name, she decided that we would name him Corky.

Corky instantly became a member of the family. He really didn't give us a choice. He would lie under the kitchen table when we ate, by our beds at night when we slept, and in the middle of the den when we were playing or watching television. He was everywhere we were.

A Yard of His Own

Corky started to get restless in our small house. Within a few days, we began putting him out for exercise in our fenced backyard. He would roam around, chase squirrels, sleep on the thick green grass in the warm sun, dig holes to nowhere, and eat. In fact, he ate a *lot!* He ate leftovers from meals, lunches we didn't like, and regular dog food. When he was bored, he would tip over a trash barrel and rummage through the garbage. He was our own personal "goat dog." We couldn't figure out why he never got sick. Dad said he had "an iron stomach," whatever that was.

The Wanderer

The fence included a wooden gate with a latch that led to the driveway. A few days after we got him, we were at school and Mom and Dad were at work when our next-door neighbor looked down from her bedroom window into our backyard and saw Corky pushing at the gate. She told us that he brought his pointed snout up and under the metal latch. After Corky's several attempts to push the latch up, the gate opened. He was free to wonder and wander the neighborhood.

Thus began the adventures of Corky the Wander Dog!

Soon afterward, Corky met his first admirer. He came across a pretty young woman moving into her new apartment. She told us that he looked excited as he trotted down our quiet street, stopping periodically to sniff the smells of other dogs, flowers, grass, and people. When he stopped to sniff her suitcase, she gave him a pat and asked him where he lived. He responded by giving her a big smile. Inviting him into her kitchen, the woman gave him food and water. The hours went by, and he made no attempt to leave. No one came looking for him, so she let him spend the night at the foot of her bed.

The next morning, she was outside her apartment unloading more boxes from her car. All of us were walking around the neighborhood, looking for Corky. Mom was talking to the pretty young woman when Corky nudged his way out of the house's side screen door and, with his twinkling brown eyes and happy grin, bounded out to meet Mom on the sidewalk. She hugged him around the neck and thanked the woman for taking care of him.

One morning Mom was home alone when the telephone rang. It was the manager of the local drugstore calling to let her know that he had Corky. Mom walked to the store, and sure enough, there was Corky with his paws up on the counter in front of the cashier. He had trotted in behind a customer and had been walking up and down the aisles. He looked at Mom as if to say, "May I help you?"

Another morning the crossing guard at the local grammar school waved him across the street and he made his way into the playground. Mom found him sitting among the children, who were talking to him and patting his sandy-colored coat. His big smile made them laugh, and Mom laughed with them!

The Escape Artist

Corky always took the opportunity to scoot around us and run out the door when Mom was leaving to go shopping. Taking off down the street, he would refuse to return when we called his name. One of us kids would shout "Shotgun!" and jump into the front seat of our van next to Mom. We would chase after Corky. It was hard when he veered off into a backyard or ran across a street. Armed with food and his leash, we would finally corner him. As if to say, "Game's over," he would slowly walk to a treat and his leash and jump up into the waiting van.

Looking for Fun

Halloween was a lot of fun. We dressed up in funny costumes and went trick-or-treating up and down the streets of our small community. One year we left Corky in the backyard with the wooden gate closed. We were two blocks from our home, running from house to house collecting candy, when Mom looked across the street. "Oh, see that cute dog walking after that group of children?" she said. "He looks like Corky."

We all turned to see him and cried, "That *is* Corky!"

Corky loved a good parade. On St. Patrick's Day, we found him with a young family. He was lying under their lawn chair, sleeping in the warm afternoon sun while the green-and-white floats went by.

After a Mardi Gras parade, we found him on the front porch of a house where college kids were having a party and had strung bright colored beads around his neck. He looked at Mom as if to say, "Come join the fun!"

Venturing Too Far

But one day, Corky's craving for adventure caught up with him. Mom and Dad were at work, and we kids were in school. Corky was bored and again nuzzled his nose under the gate latch and escaped from the yard. His usual walking route took him past the pretty woman's apartment, the crosswalk, the school playground, and the drugstore.

On this trip he decided to check out the jewelry store. The owner let him in and gave him food and water. He found our telephone number on Corky's dog tag and called our house to let us know that Corky was safe with him. No one was home. He called several times, but no one answered the telephone. He was planning to close his shop early that day. What would he do with Corky? The security guard suggested that he call the pound to have someone pick Corky up. And that's what he did.

Corky was probably frightened when a man in a blue uniform took him in a truck to a concrete building. Lots of other dogs were there in cages. He may have wondered whether we could come to pick him up.

A few hours later we found out where Corky was and came to rescue him. When he saw us, he barked and barked, jumping up and down as if to say, "Please get me out of here!" We were all excited. Mom paid the fine, and we quickly walked out with Corky on his leash as he tried to lick us all over.

After that day, Corky stayed in the backyard or the house. His wandering days were over.
There was no place like home!

Printed in the United States
By Bookmasters